D0720203

Roller-skating
as a
Spiritual Discipline

Roller-skating
as a
Spiritual Discipline

Meditations

Christopher Buice

Boston
Skinner House Books

Printed in Canada.

Cover design by Suzanne Morgan
Cover art by Patricia Frevert
Text design by WordCrafters

ISBN 1-55896-425-8

Library of Congress Cataloging-in-Publication Data

Bruice, Christopher, 1964–
    Roller-skating as a spiritual discipline : meditations /
Christopher Buice.
        p. cm.
    ISBN 1-55896-425-8 (alk. paper)
        1. Spiritual life—Meditations. I. Title

BV4501.3.B85 2002
242—dc21

                                        2001049581

10 9 8 7 6 5 4 3 2 1

05 04 03 02 01

To my wife Suzanne, and to my children, Christopher and Sarah, who have been willing to roll with the changes and have traveled full circle with me from Tennessee to Indiana to South Carolina and back to Tennessee again.

Contents

❖

Roller-skating
as a Spiritual Discipline

❖

Roller-skating is one of my spiritual disciplines. Some of
my friends don't understand what I see in this activity.
They complain that it is boring: "All you do is go around
and around in circles." And yet, this is what a spiritual
discipline is supposed to do: remind us of the cycles and
circles of life. That is why so many spiritual disciplines
are connected with holidays. Every year our holidays
remind us that we have come full circle and returned to
the place from whence we came.

Most holidays encourage a spiritual discipline. Repentance and forgiveness are practiced during the High
Holy Days of the Jewish calendar. Charity and good works
are a part of the Christmas season. Muslims fast during
the month of Ramadan. The people of the earth have
many different holidays. But we can all agree that there
are some values to which we should return each year.

I remember reading about a controversy in a small Ohio
town during the winter holidays. An avowed atheist had
put up a sign on the courthouse grounds that read,
"Once more around the sun, Happy Winter Solstice."
His sign was placed next to a manger scene set up by a
Christian community group and a menorah set up by a
Jewish organization. The county government was clearly
trying to deal with all religious groups in an evenhanded
manner. This did not stop many folks from complaining.

Although the atheist's sign was controversial, I kind of liked it. That's because I think every holiday is, in some sense, a time to say "Once more around the sun"—once more around the roller rink of life.

When I roller-skate I reflect on the many circles and cycles in which I participate. Like a planet orbiting the sun, I find myself again and again returning to the place from whence I came. And each time I do, I am a little different. The seasons leave their mark on me. I have come to understand what poet T.S. Eliot meant when he said, "The end of all our exploring will be to arrive where we started and know the place for the first time." Anyone care to skate?

A Spiritual Lesson
I Learned from My Volkswagen

❖

I learned the Hindu concept of "non-attachment to ends" from a 1974 Volkswagen Beetle. I was a teenager and it was my first car. I quickly discovered that I could not drive this particular vehicle with any certainty that I would arrive where I hoped to be. Such uncertainty could have led to frustration. However, I simply tried to learn to enjoy wherever I happened to break down.

I once made a very agreeable trip in my Volkswagen to Chattanooga, Tennessee. Of course my original destination had been Memphis. Apparently my arrival in Memphis was not meant to be. Car trouble gave me an opportunity to reconnect with an old friend from my days at summer camp. I called my pal from the garage where the car had been towed. He picked me up on his motorcycle. We drove up the windy roads to Missionary Ridge that night and stared out at the lights of the city. We talked about fond memories of the past and our hopes for the future. After a few days my car was out of the shop. I bid farewell to my friend and I was on my way back home. This Chattanooga trip was not unusual for me. It was only one of my many interesting trips to unplanned destinations.

Of course, my Beetle did not always malfunction. There were days when the engine was fine tuned and humming. I would cruise down the road with the wind in my hair and the stereo playing. These were days of perfect teenage liberty: I was an independent agent in my own automobile—although, on these days, I could not help but remind myself of the saying, "This too shall pass."

When I was sixteen years old, I prayed that I would own a car. My prayers were answered when I bought the 1974 Beetle. This is how I came to understand the meaning of the dictum, "Be careful what you pray for because you might get it." So now when I pray (or when I travel), I try not to become too attached to my desired ends. I try to enjoy the moment, appreciate the journey, and remain open about my future destination.

A Path to Greatness

❖

Being a parent is difficult work. Jesus said to the disciples, "The greatest among you shall be a servant," and I have come to the conclusion that becoming a parent is like entering boot camp for greatness. I am especially cognizant of this at mealtimes. Cooking and cleaning are only part of it. When you have small children you are always on the move. You sit down to eat. You stand up to get something the baby requires. You sit down again. You get down on your knees to retrieve an object that your beloved child has dropped on the floor. Nothing can prepare you for dinner with children. Sit down. Stand up. Get down on your knees.

An old Universalist affirmation reads, "Love is the doctrine of our church and service is our prayer." One does not have to be a parent in order to live a life of goodwill and sacrificial service. Like cells that differentiate and specialize in order to better serve the body, we are each challenged to use our own unique gifts to be of service to the larger whole of life of which we are a part. There are many different ways to contribute to the greater good, both inside and outside our homes. Discovering the gifts we have to give is one of the most meaningful challenges of life.

A life of service is a simple life. For me being a parent is an important part of that life. Others serve in equally essential ways. And as we live we often find that our joy and our service are intertwined. We discover that it is by giving that we receive. It is by emptying that we are filled. It is by losing our life that we find it. Stand up, sit down, get down on our knees. "When true simplicity is gained, to bow and to bend we shan't be ashamed. To turn, turn will be our delight, till by turning, turning we come round right." Of course, this kind of life should be freely chosen. So, if you are considering having children, don't say I didn't warn you. Today you can relax over dinner. Tomorrow you may discover that you are destined for greatness.

Should We Thank the Turkey?

❖

Thanksgiving is an awkward time for religious skeptics. It is a holiday that leads many of us to ask a distinctly theological question: "Who or what do I thank?"

In a traditional American family, everyone gathers at the table and says a prayer of thanks to God. But this is not the only way of doing things. In many hunting and gathering societies, the custom is to thank the animal itself for giving its life to become food for the family or the tribe. In this way, one could argue, the middle man is eliminated. In a polytheistic culture, a person has the difficulty of determining exactly which god to thank. The cultures of the world practice a wide variety of rituals and prayers of thanksgiving. So you do not have to feel overly self-conscious if you become a little confused at the next Thanksgiving dinner. "Should I thank God or the turkey?" you might ask yourself. A pantheist might try to eliminate the problem by saying "God is everything!" but I personally do not feel comfortable saying "God is a turkey,"at least not in front of Grandma.

Do I sound too irreverent? I hope not. I simply find the spiritual pluralism of our planet to be delightfully bewildering. The people of the world have a wide variety of theological positions. We find different answers to life's ultimate questions. On the other hand, we are all capable of sharing a deep and enduring reverence for the abundance of this natural world that sustains us. As human beings we find ourselves unable to repress our gratitude for life's many gifts. So next Thanksgiving I plan to join hands with my family and thank God for our many blessings. Of course, while no one is looking, I'll also thank the turkey.

Brothers and Sisters

❖

"Where is the toilet paper?!" This is what my friend used to holler at the top of his lungs from inside the bathroom when he was a child. The reason was that his sister used to hide the toilet paper. This was her idea of humor. She did have some compassion: After my friend had begged for a reasonable length of time, she would slide the toilet paper underneath the bathroom door, one square at a time.

Saint John once gave some difficult advice about sisters and brothers: "Those who say 'I love God' and hate their brothers and sisters are dishonest; for those who do not love a brother or sister whom they have seen, cannot love God whom they have not seen." Religious liberals have many different ideas about God. However, most of us would agree that God would never stoop so low as to hide the toilet paper from us. For this reason an unseen God may seem infinitely more lovable than a sister or brother whom we have seen (and may continue to see more frequently than we would like). Loving our brothers and sisters is not always easy. And yet, if Saint John is to be believed, it is an essential part of religious living.

I don't believe in the doctrine of original sin, but I do believe in "original sibling rivalry," the story of Cain and Abel being an example. Yet I don't need a Biblical text to prove my point. My experience as the youngest of five children has more than confirmed my belief. Still, underneath the storms and struggles of sibling rivalry, there are often deep feelings of tenderness. Through discord, conflict, and reconciliation, I have discovered that the divine and the human are intimately intertwined. I have come to understand the words of the anonymous poet:

I sought God; but God I could not see,
I sought my soul, but my soul eluded me,
I sought my brother (and sister) and found all three.

The Cashier Is My Guru

❖

The teenage cashier in a local fast food restaurant is my guru. He teaches me patience. He began his lesson by asking me to repeat my order three times. Then, after a nice long time, he handed me a bag of food that contained nothing I had ordered. After repeating my order once again and waiting another stretch of time, I finally got the food I wanted. By chance the computer was down, so I helped him do the math and calculate the correct change. When all was said and done, I had to admit that it was a very thorough and comprehensive lesson. I thanked him.

The Buddhist monks of Tibet teach that one cannot learn patience by meditating on a mountaintop or contemplating the sutras. You cannot learn this virtue even by studying with an enlightened spiritual master. The only way to learn patience is by living in the world with difficult people in inconvenient situations. That's why, at certain times, my cashier is my guru.

Patience is difficult to cultivate, and most of us do it in an uneven fashion. The challenge for religious people is to practice patience with all God's children—to extend tolerance, goodwill, and acceptance to all our fellow creatures. There are formidable obstacles to achieving this goal. The good news is that there are gurus everywhere. Remember that the next time you're waiting in line for your order.

Changing Diapers as a Religious Experience

❖

Changing diapers can be a spiritual exercise. If this activity is not one of your regular duties, then substitute another unpleasant job that you do for the benefit of those you love. It's easy to feel spiritual while sauntering through a mountain meadow, smelling wildflowers, surveying the horizon at sunset. It is more difficult to have the same spiritual feelings in the midst of a diaper change. And yet, I believe a sense of spirituality should pervade all our activities, the memorable and the mundane.

Brother Lawrence, the Christian mystic who lived in the seventeenth century, claimed that he felt closer to God when he was sweeping the floor or working in his kitchen than when he participated in Mass or formal prayers. When his hands were busy, he felt more centered and his mind was more focused. It was through his work that he was able to enter a life of prayer.

Buddhist monks teach that we will never know serenity if we wait until we complete a disagreeable task to feel at peace. There are always other jobs waiting for us after we complete our current assignment. Inevitably our peace of mind is continually postponed. Therefore, if we want to find inner peace, we must look for it in the present moment in the midst of whatever duty we are performing, however unpleasant that duty may be.

Of course, sometimes when I'm changing diapers I think that Buddhists greatly overestimate the value of the present moment. What's so great about it? And, since monks are celibate, they can avoid testing this teaching as it applies to this particular unpleasant task. And yet, I am still drawn to the power of this approach to life. I am compelled to find my peace while doing the work that is a normal part of my life.

In Sunday School I heard the story of a rabbi who gave his disciples a new commandment: "Love one another as I have loved you." That same night he wrapped a towel around his waist, filled a basin full of water, got down on his knees, and washed their feet. Washing feet is different from changing diapers. But both can be safely classified as dirty jobs. I think the rabbi was trying to teach us that love leads us to do the dirty work of life. Compassion compels us to minister to the less glamorous needs of body and soul. Reverence for life leads us to engage in the activities that nurture and sustain life. Any peace we hope to find will be discovered in these works of love, compassion, and service.

A God with Many Hands

❖

When I was a director of religious education, I took a Sunday School class to visit a local Hindu temple. There was a statue on an altar of a god with many hands. The god's arms were outstretched in all directions like the rays of a sun. The hands were open, extended, reaching out to all that lay beyond grasp—stretching to make contact with all who might need the divine touch. Many hands reaching out to those in need.

On another occasion, I saw many hands working to stock the shelves of a food pantry. These were young hands, human hands. The church youth had volunteered to work on this project to benefit the hungry in our community. Some sorted the food. Others packed grocery bags. A few took the loaded sacks to a specified area. Finally we formed a column and passed groceries down the line, out of the building, and into the back of a large truck. When the task was complete, we waved as the truck drove off. There was laughter and relaxation. We had done our job. Now the task lay in other hands.

When I became a minister of a church, I saw many hands working to rebuild Rice Chapel in Buffalo, South Carolina. All these hands working to reconstruct this African American church that had been burned down by a white arsonist. White hands. Black hands. Brown hands. Hands of many colors doing the work of healing and restoration. It was a powerful experience.

There is lots of good work that needs to be done in the world—more than any of us can do alone. That's why it is such a blessing to join together with others to achieve a worthy goal. Saint Theresa once observed, "On earth, God has no hands but our hands with which to do the work of healing." Therefore, it is good for us to band together to complete a challenging task. After all, it takes many hands to do the work of God.

The Theology School of Hard Knocks

❖

I have a theme song for roller-skating. It is by the pop group Chumbawamba. The words to the chorus are, "I get knocked down, but I get up again. You're never going to keep me down." If you have ever seen me skate, you can appreciate why this song is so appropriate.

When I put on a pair of roller skates, I sometimes feel vulnerable. I become aware that I might fall and hurt myself. If I give into fear, I will never be able to experience the fun of flying around the rink. Of course, the vulnerability I feel on roller skates is only a heightened sense of the vulnerability I feel when I am in a pair of sneakers.

Roller-skating is not the only activity during which I get knocked down. I've been knocked down on many occasions: by the death of friends and members of my family; by disappointed hopes, broken promises, and shattered dreams. I think very few of us make it around the roller rink of life completely unscathed. Many of us have learned a lesson or two from the Theology School of Hard Knocks.

One of the most significant decisions anyone can ever make is how to respond when hurt or injured by life. When I am roller-skating I realize that I have at least three choices. One temptation is simply to remain sprawled out on the roller rink floor, wallowing in my misery, hoping for some pity. Another choice is to crawl off the floor, get on the bench, nurse my wounds, and sit out the rest of the session. Or I can get up again and say, "You're never going to keep me down." In my life it has been important to make the decision to get up once more, brush myself off, and try one more time to make it around the rink. This has not always been easy. And on more than one occasion I've needed a helping hand to get me back on my feet again. Yet I know I do not want to be a permanent spectator on the sidelines of existence. In the fullness of time I want to be back in the flow of things, to re-enter and move with the rhythm of the circle of life.

The Copernican Revolution
and Other Irritating Changes

❖

"Is that it?" This was my brother Bill's response upon seeing me for the first time as a newborn baby fresh from the hospital. Apparently Mom and Dad had given me quite a buildup. "Won't it be nice to have a little brother to play with?" Bill took one look at the blob in a blanket and decided he was unimpressed.

From day one I was a disappointment to my brother. It's hardly surprising. It's not easy becoming the big brother. One minute you are the star of the show, the center of attention. Then the baby arrives and demands room in the spotlight. Suddenly you are displaced. Your parents have to divide their attention between you and the newcomer to the house. It is easy to begin to resent the new baby. I had dislodged my brother from his familiar place in the larger scheme of things.

No one likes to discover that he/she is not the center of the universe. No one likes to be displaced. Just think about what happened to Copernicus. In 1543 Copernicus began to argue that the earth was not the center of the solar system. Based on astronomical observations and mathematical theory, he developed the idea that it was the earth that revolved around the sun, not the sun that revolved around the earth. No one appreciated him very much for his efforts. Nor did Galileo win many fans when he tried to spread these ideas. Galileo was tried for heresy and forced to recant. It was not until 1992 that the Catholic Church admitted it had made a mistake by condemning him. Talk about slow progress!

Sooner or later each one of us is forced to acknowledge that we are not the center of the cosmos. We inhabit a world with other people, plants, and animals. We dwell in a universe with other stars, planets, and galaxies. At some point we are challenged to grow beyond our self-centeredness. This process is sometimes painful. Whoever helps us to learn this lesson usually doesn't win any popularity contests. The day I was born I became the bearer of unwelcome news to my brother. I, on the other hand, did not have a younger sibling to teach me this truth. Suffice it to say that my four elder siblings had ways of keeping me humble.

Do Science and Religion Need Marriage Counseling?

❖

Science and religion: Can this marriage be saved? I sometimes wonder what advice I would give to science and religion if they came to my church office in search of couple's counseling. After all, they were such a happy couple until the Middle Ages. Many early scientists were leaders in the church. But during the Renaissance they began to squabble with each other. Arguments became very heated during the Enlightenment and the scientific revolution. Now they live in different houses and sleep in separate bedrooms. One occupies the laboratory; the other inhabits churches, temples, and other religious institutions.

Some would say it was a hopeless marriage from the start. They are simply too dissimilar. They should divorce because of their irreconcilable differences. Of course, most happy couples have at least a few irreconcilable differences. I once knew a couple who had been married for over forty years. One was a Democrat and the other was a Republican. Every election day they marched off to the polls to cancel out each other's vote. You might think that it would be hard for them to live together. And yet it was a very successful marriage. Nevertheless, if you went to their house for dinner, you might hear their continuing argument over whether or not Herbert Hoover was solely responsible for causing the Great Depression.

So, irreconcilable differences do not have to lead to a divorce. If I were the designated couple's counselor for science and religion, I think I would advise them to keep talking to each other despite their separate and distinct ways of looking at the world. I think each has something to learn from the other. Science is the great discoverer of new truths and technologies. Religion gives us values and ethics so that we can use scientific discoveries for the good of all. Religion helps us to answer questions like "Who am I?" "What is my purpose in life?" Albert Einstein once observed, "Science without religion is lame. Religion without science is blind." The two could form a wonderful partnership. I would counsel science and religion to continue a dialogue with each other. Fortunately differences of opinion do not have to spell the end of a meaningful relationship.

Religion as
Legalized Gambling

❖

Churches tend to oppose state lotteries, casinos, and video poker. This is interesting because I think religion is a kind of legalized gambling. The French mathematician Pascal would have agreed with me. Long ago he argued that religion involves betting your life that there is a God. The word he used for *bet* has the same meaning as the English word for *pari-mutuel betting*. On the other hand, Pascal would have argued that being an atheist also involves a gamble. He concluded that the existence of God could not be proven or disproven on the basis of reason alone. Either theological position, belief or disbelief, is a statement of faith and involves an element of risk. The question before each person is not, "Should I gamble?" Instead it is "Which proposition should I gamble on?" One can choose either option. But either decision implies a wager. There is no escaping this game of chance. There is no way to avoid being a gambler.

Of course gambling is not confined to abstract metaphysical issues like the existence of God. It permeates all aspects of our lives and informs all of our activities. Pascal argued that if we could not act in the world except on the basis of a certainty, then we could never act because nothing is certain. Every day we act on the basis of unprovable assumptions. Will it be worth it to get out of bed tomorrow morning? We can't know for sure. And yet most of us will rise and go about our normal routine. Many acts involve an element of risk: driving on the interstate, flying in an airplane, or asking someone you love to marry you. Every act of compassion, kindness, and love is a gamble. Every effort to make the world a better place involves taking a risk.

I think church leaders are right to be concerned about some of the long-term implications of a state lottery, casinos, and legalized video poker. These are not simple questions, and they should be debated in our communities. However the question for me is not "Should we gamble?" Instead it is "For what shall we gamble?" What are we willing to risk to create a world in which there is justice, equity, and compassion in human relations? What chances are we willing to take to achieve a just and lasting peace among the nations? The life of faith always involves an element of chance. Therefore, if someone were to ask me the question, "Is religion a form of legalized gambling?" I would have to answer, "Yes, it is!" You can bet your life on it.

Grandmother's House

❖

Over the river and through Atlanta traffic to Grandmother's house we'd go. That was our routine during
various family holiday gatherings of my childhood.
I remember looking at all the food spread out on
Grandma's dining room table. There was a large turkey
roasted to a golden brown. There were salads, casseroles,
dressing, freshly baked rolls, and a variety of vegetables
to choose from. But these were of no interest to me.
There was only one dish that mattered. It was served in
a elegant fine china bowl with a ladle to the side. It was
a delicious, piping hot bowl of spaghettios. I was always
excited to see that Grandma had cooked my favorite
dish. She had lovingly opened the can, poured the con-
tents into a pot, and warmed them to perfection. And,
of course, there was the "presentation." I am probably
one of the few people on earth who has been served
spaghettios from the finest china.

My grandmother was a Southern Baptist. My father,
her son, became an Episcopal priest. I am a Unitarian
Universalist minister. (Perhaps this is the trickle-down
theory operating in religion.) Grandma died before I
became a member of a UU church. I am not sure how
she would have reacted. Perhaps she would have felt the
same as my aunt, who once exclaimed to my brother
Sam, "Chris is a Unitarian?! I thought he was at least an

Episcopalian." This was not a diplomatic comment, considering that Sam is an Episcopal priest.

Would my grandmother be surprised by my choices? Maybe not. Grandma taught me from earliest childhood that there is room at the table for someone who is a little bit different from the rest. The memory of that bowl of spaghettios continually reminds me to make room in my heart for people who are a bit odd in their tastes and dispositions. There can be room in our hearts for diversity. There can be a place at the table for everyone, even the more finicky children of God.

The Bible and Bigfoot

❖

There is a controversy among those who search for Bigfoot. The debate centers around a famous 1967 amateur film that shows Sasquatch sauntering away from a river. This movie has long endured the close examination of critics and helped to bolster the faith of Bigfoot believers. One such examination, however, threatened to upset the apple cart. Two researchers took a close-up look at the movie, frame by frame. They zoomed in and magnified the details of each shot. After careful study, they determined that they could just make out what appeared to be a zipper. The two concluded that the film was possibly a fraud and that the creature in the picture might not be anything more than a man in a monkey suit.

Oddly enough, the two researchers were not skeptics who set out to debunk the myth of Bigfoot. The two believed in Bigfoot. They continue to do so in spite of their conclusion that the film is a fraud. Unfortunately these researchers found themselves ostracized by many in the community of Sasquatch seekers. Their views unsettled the basis of faith among many of their colleagues. Friendships went bust. Coworkers were estranged. Two people were cast out of the fold.

I think the free and responsible search for truth and meaning is like the quest for Bigfoot. If you've ever traveled in the Northwest wilderness, then you know there is room for the hidden and the unknown. I think our ideas about the mysteries of life should be open to scrutiny and careful examination. For better and/or worse, I am the kind of guy who looks at my beliefs frame by frame, magnifying and zooming in on the details, examining the nuances and subtleties. I think my beliefs should be able to hold up under close inspection. It doesn't matter if an idea is found in the Bible or in a Bigfoot film. I believe a good idea will hold up under close scrutiny. Engaging in this process does not always help me to win friends and influence people. And yet, I think this is the best way to engage in the search for truth and meaning in life. Nor is it a bad way to go about looking for Bigfoot.

Disorganized Religion

❖

"I don't believe in organized religion," I once said. That was before I found the Unitarian Universalist Church. Of course, those who have seen my minister's study claim I still do not believe in organized religion. When I was a director of religious education, I was once asked to state my philosophy of administration. I responded, "I organize a Sunday School in much the same way as one might go about inciting a riot: I get everyone excited and hope it happens." This philosophy served me well during my tenure as an RE director. Something of that spirit carries over into my work in the parish ministry.

I don't mean to totally dismiss the importance of detailed management. I am conscientiously striving to grow in this area. Day by day, I learn more about the importance of a carefully implemented strategy for church administration. But I also appreciate the value of spontaneity and creative chaos.

Many people like their churches to be well organized. Centuries of theology have given us the picture of a God who makes order out of chaos. And yet, this theology does not serve us well when the choir hits a wrong note, or a baby gurgles loudly, or the pianist plays an octave too high, or a child crawls under the pews, or someone fails to turn on the microphone, or the minister forgets to introduce the second hymn.

When we think of God as the power that brings order out of chaos, we become upset with the occasional and unavoidable disorderliness of everyday life. We forget that creative power often involves a measure of messiness. That is why I like to think of God as love. Love is like a prophet that turns over tables in my temple, disturbing all my notions of order and upsetting all the rituals and theologies that interfere with my ability to love my neighbor as myself. This is not to say that I do not do my best to run a tight ship on Sunday morning. It is only to say that sometimes I gain my clearest understanding of the divine when chaos is made out of my order.

Bless You

❖

Being a parent gives one many opportunities to "bless them that curse you." Yes, this advice from the Sermon on the Mount comes in handy when you are serving vegetables, enforcing curfews, or suggesting alternatives to watching television. If you are not a parent, perhaps you've learned a similar skill in your workplace, home, or church. It is difficult to please the ones you love all the time.

When I was a child, I learned a lot from my mother about how to deal with an adversary. On one occasion I asked Mom if I could have a chocolate cream snack cake. She said, "No, it will spoil your supper." This made me terribly angry, and so I did the only logical thing—I ran away from home. I didn't pack any bags. I just hit the door and started walking through the woods. Unfortunately there was a flaw in my plan. Generally it is not a good idea to run away from home on an empty stomach. This occurred to me when, a few minutes later, I heard my mother calling off in the distance, "Christopher, it's time to eat."

When I returned home, I was disappointed to discover that no one had even realized that I had left the house. The prodigal son returned home and no one ever noticed he'd been away. Fortunately there was a fine meal waiting for me anyway. I participated gladly in my homecoming feast. After dinner I was not angry with

Mom anymore. I even gave her a kiss at bedtime. My mother knew something about peacemaking. Insomuch as she was able, she strove to live peaceably with her children. When her enemies were hungry, she fed them. When they were thirsty, she gave them something to drink. My mother knew how to love her enemies.

Cosmic Bowling

❖

I think about the Buddha when I am bowling. A bowling ball that goes too far to the right ends up in the gutter. One that drifts to the left experiences a similar fate. And so, when bowling I am aware that I am seeking the Middle Way.

The Buddha sought the Middle Way between body-destroying asceticism and gluttonous indulgence of the appetites and cravings. Either extreme took him away from spiritual growth. I, too, realize that it is important to seek a middle way between the extremes of life: between firmness and flexibility, realism and hope, charity and empowerment. The Middle Way is a difficult path to tread. The Hindu scriptures, the Upanishads, warn us that the path to salvation is as thin and narrow as a razor's edge. Fortunately a bowling lane is somewhat wider.

Finding the middle way is often difficult. On some occasions I feel as if bowling lanes are far too narrow. I long for a wider margin of error. Unfortunately this is not always possible. Sure, I can have kiddy bumpers placed in the gutters, but that feels like cheating. I find that my greatest satisfaction comes not from trying to change the game but from changing myself. By centering my ball to glide down the lane, I find that my life becomes more centered with the Larger Life of which I am a part. By focusing my energies toward a central goal, I find a sense of precision and balance in my life

And yet, the way to live a centered or balanced life is not always obvious. It is not always easy to find the middle way between two extremes. That is why I sometimes wish for a wider lane in my bowling alley. I roll a lot of gutter balls when I bowl. But I find that it is by accepting life on life's terms that I truly begin to enjoy the game. History tells us that it took many, many years for the Buddha to achieve enlightenment. While I am waiting, I might as well continue bowling.

Dead White Males

❖

Feminists reject the presentation of Western history as the story of DWMs, or Dead White Males. This point is valid. (But I cannot condemn all Dead White Males categorically, partially because I expect I will be one in the fullness of time.) Women scholars remind us that the world looks different through female eyes.

One of my favorite feminist thinkers is my six-year-old daughter Sarah. She is a born feminist. Since birth she has been educating me about how girls see the world. From her earliest years, she has questioned the way things are. While I was reading a book to her at bedtime she would ask, "Where are the girls in this story?" Her question forced me to think about things. It made me realize that there is, indeed, a shortage of powerful women characters in early childhood books. Often the women characters serve as mere window dressing to accent the actions of powerful men. My daughter has never approved of this aspect of children's literature. And so, sometimes when I am reading, Sarah will ask me to change the gender of one of the main characters of the story, in order to makes things more inclusive. And I am always happy to comply with her request—even though sometimes I end up a bit tongue-tied in my efforts to do so.

Some might question my willingness to perform a sex-change operation on a fictional character. Doesn't this interfere with the artist's intent? Maybe so . . . and yet I see this action as an effort to make the world a better place. It is my effort to respond to my child's questions and concerns—to open up her imagination to a world of new possibilities. One day I will no doubt be a DWM. Until then I can do my best to make things more fair for my daughter and the other strong women of the world.

A Walk in the Woods

❖

Walking in the woods helps me to keep perspective. On some parts of one of my favorite trails I have the opportunity to walk beside a clear mountain stream while the continual and abiding sound of cascading water fills my ears. On other parts of the trail I can walk around enormous boulders, remnants of the Ice Age. Walking by these stones I begin to empathize with the way ants must feel. I begin to feel somehow smaller and less significant, like a very tiny and new thing in a world of older, larger, and more enduring realities.

When you begin a hike, it's easy to feel that your personal troubles are the most important things in the world. But it is difficult to maintain that perspective. As you walk along the trail and become enveloped in the sights and sounds of the forest, human problems become human sized again. Worries seem smaller in an environment in which things keep humming and buzzing and moving and growing regardless of how your job search is going, how much you owe on your house or car, or how worried you are about your health.

One of the things I've noticed is that nature does not worry. We human beings do worry. Often we make mountains out of molehills. We make small problems into issues of life or death. But in the forest issues of life and death are ever-present. And yet no creature, no plant, no tree, no flower seems to worry about it. A wise rabbi once said, "Consider the lilies of the field; they do not toil neither do they spin, and yet Solomon in all his glory was not clothed as one of these." For brief periods of time as I walk through the forest, my mind is able to stop its toiling and spinning and worrying, and I surrender to the music of all the life that surrounds me: the songs of birds, the chirping of crickets, the melody of the creek. At these moments I realize that the sound of my own heartbeat is only one note in the symphony of life and that on that inevitable day, sometime in the future, when this heartbeat stops, the music will continue. The symphony will be undiminished.

A Trip to the Mosque

❖

"What do Muslims imagine God to look like?" The question was asked by a young boy in our Unitarian Universalist Sunday School class when we were visiting the local mosque. We were meeting together with a Muslim religious education class. A young girl from the mosque replied, "There is a saying in our religion: 'Whatever you imagine God to be, he is the opposite.' And so if you then imagine God to be the opposite of the thing you first imagined, you must imagine that God is the opposite of that. Or, in other words, there is no way for us to know what God looks like." Another student, a Muslim boy, said, "God is a being that is neither male nor female but, like many other religions, we use the word *He.*" And another student said, "We have a saying in our tradition that 'You cannot see God with your outer eye, but you can see him with the inner eye,' or you can see God in the orderliness of the universe."

After the question and answer session was over, we went into the main room, where an Imam led the prayers in Arabic. The assembled worshipers were from Africa, India, Persia, the Middle East, and America. People from all over the earth were bowing in the same direction and worshiping the same God. After the prayers we reassembled in the classroom, where we discovered that Unitarian Universalist kids and Muslim kids share common ground in the love of doughnuts. The people at the mosque were warm and friendly. I talked with one youth about his experience fasting during the month of Ramadan. After our social time, a leader from the mosque gave the class a beautifully bound hardback copy of the Koran, written in Arabic with an English translation, as a gift to our church. When I left the mosque with that copy of the Koran in my arms, I was aware that it was only one of many gifts I had received during my visit.

Eulogy for a Honda

❖

The other day my little Honda gave up the ghost on the side of the highway. I, of course, went through the predictable stages of grief. First I was in denial: Surely, if I just turned the key one more time. . . . Then I went into the stage called *bargaining*. I told my mechanic, "Do whatever it takes to save her! Spare no expense!" My mechanic, in his best carside manner, assured me that it was a lost cause. Finally I came to the last stage, called *acceptance*. I cleaned out the car, removed all of my belongings, canceled the insurance, and removed the license plate.

This Honda and I had been through a lot together. I was a young, single man, fresh out of college, when I first got the car. Now I am a husband and the father of two children. I drove this car to work at five different jobs in three different states. My car got me through some tight times. If my car had broken down when I was in seminary studying for the ministry, it would have thrown my family into a financial tailspin. It didn't. It saw us through.

I told the people of my first church that I would have to continue to drive my Honda until I paid off my student loans from theology school. This was a bit unrealistic, considering it was fifteen years old with over 210,000 miles. My car was reliable but not immortal. I suppose it may seem a little self-indulgent to grieve the loss of a car.

There are far greater losses. Then again, it may also be true that losing a car puts us in touch with the residual sadness we feel about other times we've had to let go. It may even cause us to think ahead to the day we all know we must face—the day when one of our own internal parts gives way. Something breaks or bursts and our journey on this earth comes to halt, on the side of some road, in the midst of some journey.

My car was an inanimate object. It was a material thing. And yet, I can't help but feel a certain gratitude for this particular machine. In this unpredictable and uncertain world, there is one less thing I can depend on. And so I've written this eulogy for an 1984 Honda Accord: "Well done, good and faithful servant. You have poured yourself out like an offering and the time has come for your departure. You've fought the good fight. You've finished the race. Goodbye."

Heaven and Hell
at the Breakfast Table

❖

Breakfast is an interesting experience in our household. Sometimes it's heaven. Sometimes it's hell. Some days we are friendly to each other. We pass the milk. No one hogs the cereal box. All is tranquil. Other mornings things go badly. Everyone is rushed. Things are chaotic. We are running behind schedule. People are not on their best behavior.

Breakfast is my first encounter of the day with fellow members of the human race. The interactions I experience at breakfast can set the tone for my whole day. This is because I tend to take my relationships with me wherever I go. If things are going well at home, then all is well with the world. If my family is experiencing domestic bliss, then peace pervades everywhere. On the other hand, if there is disharmony at breakfast, then I take it with me to work and anywhere else I might go that day. If breakfast is hell and I try to escape breakfast turmoil by leaving the room or the house, it doesn't work. I usually take a feeling of discord with me. There seems to be no way to elude the ties that bind.

In many ways I feel the same about my relationship to my family as the author of the Book of Psalms felt about his relationship to God.

> Whither shall I go from thy spirit?
> or whither shall I flee from thy presence?
> If I ascend up into heaven, thou art there;
> if I make my bed in hell, behold, thou art there.

Sometimes I ask myself, "Whither shall I go to flee from my relationships—whether they be with my family, friends, or coworkers? Whither shall I go to escape my ties to my neighbors—whether they be rich or poor, male or female, gay or straight; red, brown, yellow, black or white?" For we are all members of one family, related to each other and to the Divine. We are all gathered around the common table of Creation. The way we relate to each other may mean the difference between heaven and hell. I do not believe that salvation is an escape from our relationships. It is not about simply waiting for some heaven or bliss in the hereafter. I believe that salvation can be the experience of peace, goodwill, and reconciliation in the here and now in the context of our relationships. For, if we do not experience salvation in the present moment, then we are unlikely to find it wherever we may go.

Interfaith Dialogue
through Play-doh

❖

A number of years ago I helped to organize an exhibition by a group of Tibetan Buddhist monks who were touring the country. These monks were here to demonstrate the Tibetan art of butter sculpture. I didn't know anything about butter sculpture at the time, but I was glad to help organize the event.

Part of my responsibility was to find home hospitality for the monks. One local family with two small children agreed to host two of the monks. The couple was a little nervous because the Tibetans did not speak English well and the couple did not speak Tibetan at all. Of course their fears turned out to be unwarranted. The Tibetan monks were wonderful guests. They found nonverbal ways of communicating.

During their visit the monks happened to notice the two small children playing with play-doh. The monks got down with the children and started playing with them. The Tibetans and the children played together, molding many different shapes and combining various colors. It turned out that play-doh was a lot like the material the monks use for their butter sculpture. So the children and the monks discovered that they liked to play with the same stuff. They laughed and had fun together. They were able to overcome differences of culture, language,

age, and religion through their common enjoyment of play-doh.

Adults communicate with words. We often write down what we have to say in letters, books, essays, and articles. But any child psychologist will tell you that play is the language of childhood. Play is how children communicate with each other and make sense of the world. Some theologians would even say that play is how children learn to participate in that larger Creativity in which we live and move and have our being. Theologians and psychologists agree that play is a meaningful activity. Adult Christians look to the Bible for meaning, Muslims to the Koran, Hindus to the Vedas, and Buddhists to the Sutras. But children of all faiths find meaning and renewal through play. For them (and for us) play can lead to the renewal of mind, body, and spirit.

Repent or Perish

❖

When I was a camp counselor at YMCA Camp Ocoee, we used to drive twenty miles into Cleveland, Tennessee, whenever we got a break from work. This was our chance to eat in a restaurant and catch a movie. As we drove into town we were greeted by a sign posted on the side of the road: "Repent or Perish." This message helped to set a cheerful note for our weekend activities.

Many years later I began studying theology and I discovered that the word *repent* has many meanings. One of the meanings of repent is literally "turn around." Had I known that earlier, I'm sure I would have turned my car around at the Cleveland city limits and gone back to camp.

Another meaning of the word *repent* is the Jewish concept of *teshuva*. This kind of repentance means that we change our personal priorities in life and pick a new positive direction. We let go of our bad habits and egocentric thinking, and we move in the direction of working for the common good of all people and creation.

I sometimes think of that sign outside of Cleveland when I contemplate the problems of our world. If we are to protect the environment of our planet, we will need a new ordering of priorities and a change in values. We will need to give up some bad habits from our past. Pollution in our water, air, land, and food serves as a reminder that we need to change course if we want to go forward. Or, as the sign told us, we need to "repent or perish."

Moses, Me, and
the Meaning of Ministry

❖

What is a minister? My favorite definition comes from the learned theologian Urban Holmes. He wrote that a minister is a person who acts as a "bridge by which the community links its formal and empirical comprehension with its intuited sense of myth and metaphor." I think that definition makes everything perfectly clear. Is there any need for me to continue this meditation? What more could I add?

Just in case there are some folks who are not completely satisfied with that definition, let me try to define ministry by telling you a story. It is a story about Moses and the Hebrew people. They had escaped from slavery in Egypt, but they had not quite made it to the Promised Land. They were on the move through the wilderness and they needed a place to worship. It couldn't be a temple made of stones. It had to be portable. They needed a spiritual mobile home. And so Moses told the Hebrew people to bring out gifts of blue and purple and red yarn. He asked for gifts of fine linen, goat hair, and ram skins. And then craftsmen used the gifts that had been given to fashion a tent that would serve as a temple, a house of worship.

I see ministry as the work of the whole community. I agree with the Quakers that the task of an egalitarian church is not to abolish the ministry; it is to abolish the laity—to empower everyone for the work of shared ministry. We must work together to call forth the gifts of all the people. Gifts of music, teaching, social action, celebration, caring, creativity, and more. Like skilled craftspeople, we can weave these gifts together into one cloth in order to create a big tent . . . the Beloved Community . . . a chapel of all faiths. Stones and wood can make a building. It takes the gifts of the people to build a church and a ministry. Let's start building!

Gem Mining

❖

A few summers ago my wife Suzanne and I took our son Christopher gem mining in the mountains of North Carolina. We mounded a pile of mud and dirt, got a sifter, and began sifting through the soil in search of treasure.

Liberal religious education is like gem mining. In a Unitarian Universalist Sunday School we endeavor to teach our children discernment. The word *discernment* comes from the Latin word *discernere,* which means "to separate," "to distinguish," "to sort out." In other words, we try to teach our children how to be gem miners. The process of gem mining is simple. You take some dirt, place it into a strainer, run creek water through it, and sift until you find a gem.

Liberal religious gem mining requires the ability to discern what is worth keeping and what should be sifted out and discarded. This can be difficult. Our children have to sift through lots of information in life. They learn values from television, popular music, the Internet, books, magazines, their friends, and many other sources. We can't even know all the messages they are exposed to on a regular basis.

We cannot shelter our children forever. But we can teach them the process of discernment and the art of gem mining. We can help to awaken the conscience so that they will be able make responsible choices, to separate things of value from things that have no value. At some point we must open the door and lead our children into the world and speak the words to them that tradition says God spoke to the children of Israel: "I have set before you life and death, a blessing and a curse. Therefore choose life."

Are You Saved?

❖

Occasionally I am stopped on the street and asked the question, "Are you saved?" Even though I am a minister, I am never sure how to reply. Then I remember a story from my own childhood. When I was a child, four or five years old, I took my brother's pocket knife and began carving some words into the wooden headboard of my bed. When my mother discovered my creative work, she was justifiably angry. I think normally vandalism of furniture would have gotten me into deep trouble. But my mother was a minister's wife, and the words I had carved into the bed were "Jesus Loves Me." In this kind of situation it is true that "Jesus saves."

Of course I was saved not only by Jesus. I was saved by a mom who knew how to balance accountability with forgiveness. I imagine that it is difficult to know how to discipline your children when their religious expression does damage to the furniture. But through a gentle talk, my mom was able to help me see the error of my ways and I changed my behavior for the better.

Another time I was saved when I was swimming in the ocean. I went out into water way over my head and was caught in the undertow. Fortunately my brother Sam noticed that I was struggling. He jumped into the water and came out to get me. He hauled me in to shore. Once again I was saved by a grace, both human and divine.

When I hear the word *saved,* I think of being rescued from danger, delivered from evil, protected from harm. And in many ways I have been saved. Sometimes this experience of salvation has a human hand and a person's face. At other times I encounter it when I am alone in the woods and there is no sound except the whispering of the wind playing in the leaves or water flowing over rocks in a stream. And as I remember these things I know the answer to the question, "Are you saved?" "Yes," I reply, "I am definitely saved."

A Memory of Youth

❖

I remember, when I was about fifteen years old, going to a conference of Episcopal youth groups at Camp Michael in North Georgia. I had been looking forward to the retreat, but when I got there I was disappointed. Every minute of the weekend was packed with classes and activities. There was no time to get away from structured sessions. There was no time for silence or solitude.

All the structure began to bother me. I began to wonder what religion would be like if there weren't any books or classes or words. I began to wonder if religion was something I would have discovered in the world if I had never been to Sunday School or had never been taught anything about it. I began to wish I had more time alone to think about these things.

And so, on Saturday afternoon some friends and I slipped away from the activities to go on a hike. We walked up a mountain. The mountain was fairly small but the trail was steep. I remember being out of breath when we reached the summit. At the top there was a big rock to sit on. From our perch we had a beautiful view of the valley below us. It was a wonderful sight.

We sat there on the rock and we were all quiet. I remember the silence and the gentle breeze and the feeling of being all alone even though I was among friends. It was there on the rock, far away from the books and classes and words, that I gained a sense of wholeness and peace. In the stillness I felt something powerful.

Perhaps it is this feeling that is our connection to God and meaning. Perhaps it is this feeling that all the books, classes, cathedrals, synagogues, temples, mosques, and other human inventions are struggling to find and then to exalt and celebrate. I don't know. All I do know is that on a mountaintop, when I was fifteen years old, I felt something.

Unitarian Universalist
Meditation Manuals

Unitarians and Universalists have been publishing annual editions of prayer collections and meditation manuals for 150 years. In 1841 the Unitarians broke with their tradition of addressing only theological topics and published *Short Prayers for the Morning and Evening of Every Day in the Week, with Occasional Prayers and Thanksgivings.* Over the years, the Unitarians published many volumes of prayers, including Theodore Parker's selections. In 1938 *Gaining a Radiant Faith* by Henry H. Saunderson launched the current tradition of an annual Lenten manual.

Several Universalist collections appeared in the early nineteenth century. A comprehensive *Book of Prayers* was published in 1839, featuring both public and private devotions. During the late 1860s, the Universalist Publishing House was founded to publish denominational materials. Like the Unitarians, the Universalists published Lenten manuals, and in the 1950s they complemented this series with Advent manuals.

Since 1961, the year the Unitarians and the Universalists consolidated, the Lenten manual has evolved into a meditation manual, reflecting the theological diversity of the two denominations. Today the Unitarian Universalist Association meditation manuals include two styles of collections: poems or short prose pieces written by one author—usually a Unitarian Universalist minister—and anthologies of works by many authors.